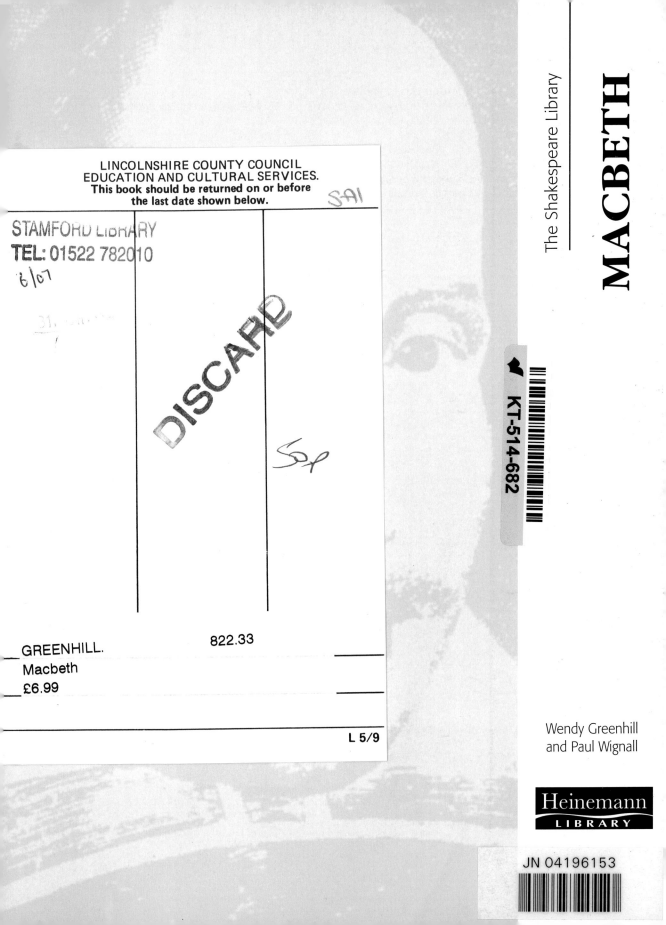

The Shakespeare Library

MACBETH

Wendy Greenhill
and Paul Wignall

Heinemann
LIBRARY

H **www.heinemann.co.uk/library**
Visit our website to find out more information about Heinemann Library books.

To order:
☎ Phone 44 (0) 1865 888112
🖹 Send a fax to 44 (0) 1865 314091
🖥 Visit the Heinemann bookshop at **www.heinemann.co.uk/library** to browse our catalogue and order online.

First published in Great Britain by Heinemann Library, Halley Court, Jordan Hill, Oxford OX2 8EJ, part of Harcourt Education.
Heinemann is a registered trademark of Harcourt Education Ltd.

Editorial: Clare Lewis
Design: Dave Poole and Geoff Ward
Picture Research: Melissa Allison
Production: Helen McCreath

Printed and bound in China by WKT

13 digit ISBN 978 0 431 07634 8 (hardback)
10 09 08 07 06
10 9 8 7 6 5 4 3 2 1

13 digit ISBN 978 0 431 07811 3 (paperback)
11 10 09 08 07
10 9 8 7 6 5 4 3 2 1

British Library Cataloguing in Publication Data
Greenhill, Wendy and Wignall, Paul
Macbeth – 2nd ed. – (The Shakespeare library)
822.3'3
A full catalogue record for this book is available from the British Library.

Acknowledgements
The publishers would like to thank the following for permission to reproduce photographs: Bridgeman Art Library, p6; The British Library, p4; Cambridge University Library, p7; Corbis/Robbie Jack pp13, 27; Photostage/Donald Cooper pp8, 9, 15, 16; ET Archive, pp5, 24; RSC Collection, pp19, 21, 28; Shakespeare Centre Library/Joe Cocks Studio Collection, pp10, 11, 17, 23, 27, 29; Tate Gallery, p12; Victoria and Albert Museum, pp14, 18, 20.

Cover photograph reproduced with permission of Corbis/Scot Frei.

The publishers would like to thank Dr Paul Edmondson, Head of Education at the Shakespeare Birthplace Trust, for his assistance in the preparation of this book.

Every effort has been made to contact copyright holders of any material reproduced in this book. Any omissions will be rectified in subsequent printings if notice is given to the publishers.

CONTENTS

Introduction: pleasing a king　　　　　　　　　　**4**

The sources　　　　　　　　　　**6**

The characters　　　　　　　　　　**8**

What happens　　　　　　　　　　**10**

The themes　　　　　　　　　　**14**

Past productions　　　　　　　　　　**18**

Actors' perspectives: playing Macbeth　　　　　　　　　　**20**

Actors' perspectives: playing Lady Macbeth　　　　　　　　　　**24**

The Weird Sisters and the Porter　　　　　　　　　　**28**

Glossary　　　　　　　　　　**30**

More books to read & Websites　　　　　　　　　　**31**

Index　　　　　　　　　　**32**

Any words appearing in the text in bold, **like this** are explained in the glossary.

INTRODUCTION

❖ pleasing a king ❖

William Shakespeare was a professional actor, a businessman, and a playwright. Today, nearly 400 years after his death, his plays are still performed, moving audiences to tears and to laughter. Shakespeare's works tell us much about **Elizabethan** England. What is most remarkable is that Shakespeare's plays can still tell us something about ourselves.

In 1603, William Shakespeare and his colleagues at the Globe theatre were at the height of their popularity. Known as the Chamberlain's Men, they were under the protection of the **Lord Chamberlain**, the organizer of entertainment at **court**. The Chamberlain's Men were often asked to play for Queen Elizabeth I. The Lord Chamberlain was a man of power in the world of plays and **playhouses**. His office granted companies licences to perform. He demanded changes to plays if he thought they would offend the Queen. He could even have actors and writers imprisoned. Generally, though, the Chamberlain's Men knew how to keep on the right side of those in power.

A new reign

Queen Elizabeth I died childless at Richmond-on-Thames on 24 March 1603. News travelled fast. By 5 April, her successor, King James VI of Scotland, was leaving Edinburgh to be crowned King James I of England. James became King of Scotland at the age of three when Elizabeth had **deposed** his mother, Mary Queen of Scots. He was widely read and wrote poetry and books on many subjects. He was determined to be a wise and firm king.

BELOW: This is the **frontispiece** to King James I's book from 1597, *Daemonologie*.

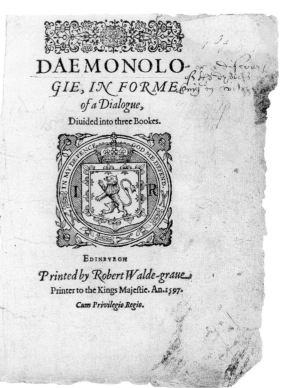

DAEMONOLO-GIE, IN FORME of a Dialogue, Diuided into three Bookes.

EDINBVRGH
Printed by Robert Walde-graue
Printer to the Kings Maiestie. An. 1597.
Cum Privilegio Regio.

ABOVE: These are the conspirators in the Gunpowder Plot of 1605.

Shortly after arriving in London, James took the Chamberlain's Men under his wing and renamed them the King's Men. They played before the King about 10 times a year, and they relied on his support and protection.

During his 35-year reign in Scotland, James had learned how to survive plots, **rebellions**, and riots. He was terrified that he would be assassinated, so he wore specially padded clothes for protection. King James had good reason to be concerned. Within two years, there were several plots to kill him. The most famous was the Gunpowder Plot of 1605. The conspirators were all Roman Catholics. The official religion of England was Protestant, and many feared that Catholic Spain would take over England. James was convinced that he had been chosen by God to be king and that anyone plotting against him must be in league with the devil.

Witchcraft was also seen as a real threat to society. In fact, James had written a book about it in 1597, called *Daemonologie*. The king saw witches and Catholic plotters as two of his greatest enemies.

Macbeth

Macbeth was probably written in early 1606, when plots against the king seemed to be everywhere. In his play, Shakespeare presents a man who is told by three witches that he will be king. The man is then encouraged by his wife to fulfill the **prophecy** by killing the king. This is what the real King James feared most. But *Macbeth* was not written just to please the King. It is a play that also asks many difficult questions about ambition, guilt, conscience, and the nature of evil.

THE SOURCES

Early in his career, while Elizabeth was on the throne, Shakespeare had written a series of plays about English history. They had shown England torn apart by civil war. This conflict was called the Wars of the Roses. The civil war ended when Henry Tudor, Queen Elizabeth I's grandfather, became King Henry VII. Shakespeare showed that Elizabeth's family, the Tudors, had the best claim to the throne, both legally and morally.

Shakespeare's history plays make great use of Raphael Holinshed's *Chronicles of England, Scotland and Ireland*. The book was so popular that it was printed in 1577 and then printed again in an expanded version in 1587. In 1606, with the new king to please, Shakespeare opened his copy of Holinshed once more. He turned to the story of the murder of King Duncan of Scotland and the evil reign of Macbeth.

Building the plot

Shakespeare does not simply repeat Holinshed's story, in which Macbeth and Banquo conspire to assassinate King Duncan. The real king, King James, claimed to be descended from Banquo. To connect him with King Duncan's killer would not be looked upon favourably. So Shakespeare drew on another Scottish story from the Holinshed book – the murder of King Duff.

RIGHT: This portrait of King James I was painted by John de Critz in 1610.

Duff was murdered while he was a guest in his assassin's house. From this, and from another version of the Macbeth story in George Buchanan's *History of Scotland*, Shakespeare found the character of Lady Macbeth, the woman who pushed her husband to commit murder.

Shakespeare's own reading of the Latin plays of Seneca, and his knowledge about witchcraft, guilty consciences, and plots to overthrow the king, add to his story of *Macbeth*. However, part of Shakespeare's plan was to present King James as the rightful king of England, and to show James as a good and wise ruler.

In August 1606, Shakespeare's company probably performed the play *Macbeth*, before King James and King Christian I of Denmark. It is not known for sure if this was its first performance, though it is likely. It was certainly performed on the outdoor stage of the Globe theatre in London, where it was seen in April 1611 by Simon Forman, a London doctor and astrologer. This performance is known because Forman described it in his book titled *Book of Plays*.

In writing *Macbeth*, Shakespeare was, as usual, adapting material from several sources. He did not simply use history as found in the Holinshed's *Chronicles*, but instead wrote a story that would flatter and interest the king. He had learned how to please an audience and how to survive in dangerous times.

BELOW: This engraving from Holinshed's *Chronicles*, 1577, shows Macbeth, Banquo, and the witches.

THE CHARACTERS

THREE **WEIRD** SISTERS Witches who foretell that Macbeth will be king and that Banquo will be the father of kings

KING DUNCAN OF SCOTLAND Murdered by Macbeth

MALCOLM Duncan's eldest son, who escapes to England after his father's murder. Later, he becomes Prince of Cumberland.

DONALBAIN Duncan's younger son, who escapes to Ireland after his father's death

A CAPTAIN Serves in Duncan's army and describes Macbeth's bravery in battle

MACBETH **Thane** of Glamis. He will be made Thane of Cawdor. He becomes King of Scotland after he murders Duncan.

LADY MACBETH Macbeth's wife

BANQUO A Scottish thane. At first he is Macbeth's friend and fellow general. Later he is murdered on Macbeth's orders.

FLEANCE Banquo's son, who escapes when his father is killed

MACDUFF Thane of Fife. He kills Macbeth in the last battle.

LADY MACDUFF Murdered on Macbeth's orders

MACDUFF'S SON Murdered with his mother

LENNOX, ROSS, ANGUS, CAITHNESS, MENTEITH Scottish thanes

A Porter Gatekeeper at Macbeth's castle

Seyton Macbeth's servant

Three Murderers

A Doctor Attends to Lady Macbeth

A Woman Servant to Lady Macbeth

Siward An English lord, Earl of Northumberland

Young Siward Siward's son, killed by Macbeth in the last battle

An English Doctor

Hecate Queen of the witches

Three More Witches Companions of Hecate

Three Apparitions:

A Head

A Bloody Child

A Child Wearing a Crown

A Spirit Like a Cat

Other Spirits

A procession of Eight Kings

An Old Man, A Messenger, Murderers, Servants, and Soldiers

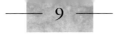

RIGHT: David Troughton played the Porter in the Royal Shakespeare Company's 1987 production.

WHAT HAPPENS

The Weird Sisters meet

The play opens with a short but spectacular scene of the three witches meeting in thunder and lightning to arrange their next gathering. They decide to get together later that day, after the battle on a **heath** where they know they will find MACBETH.

The Rebellion Is Crushed

Two Scottish **thanes**, Macdonald and Cawdor, have rebelled against their king with help from the King of Norway. KING DUNCAN has sent an army led by his loyal thanes to defeat them. News reaches Duncan that the battle is won.

The hero of the day is Macbeth, who killed the traitor Macdonald. Duncan gives orders that Cawdor is to be executed and that Macbeth will be rewarded with his title and position.

Macbeth and the Weird Sisters

The three witches meet and exchange stories of torments. When Macbeth and BANQUO stumble across them, the witches greet Macbeth calling him by three titles: Thane of Glamis, which he is; Thane of Cawdor, which he doesn't yet understand; and the future king. Banquo is hailed as the founder of a line of kings. The witches vanish. ROSS and ANGUS, messengers from King Duncan, arrive. They praise Macbeth and confer on him the title Thane of Cawdor. Banquo is cautious in believing the truth of the witches' **prophecy**. Macbeth is more deeply affected. Has he already been dreaming about being king?

RIGHT: Macbeth, Banquo, and the witches in a scene from the Royal Shakespeare Company's 1976 production of *Macbeth*.

ABOVE: The majestic King Duncan is surrounded by his Court in the 1976 Royal Shakespeare Company production.

Malcolm is named heir

Duncan presides over a gathering of all his thanes and his two sons, MALCOLM and DONALBAIN. Macbeth and Banquo are honoured for their bravery. Then Duncan announces that he has chosen his eldest son, Malcolm, as his heir. Macbeth realizes that this blocks his ambition for more power. The royal party sets out for Macbeth's castle at Inverness. This is a sign that King Duncan favours Macbeth, as it was an honour to have the king as a guest in one's castle.

Lady Macbeth's ambition

At Macbeth's castle in Inverness, LADY MACBETH receives a letter from her husband about the witches' prophecy. She begins to plot. She doubts that Macbeth is able to carry out the violent actions necessary to achieve his ambitions. She calls on spirits to replace all womanly gentleness and pity with "direst cruelty". When Macbeth arrives, she speaks the unspeakable: Duncan is not to leave their castle alive. She urges her husband to be cunning and deceitful. She wants the king's crown for him. Macbeth is less certain. Duncan arrives, and Lady Macbeth greets him graciously.

The murder

Macbeth is plagued by his conscience. He knows that their plan is wrong, and he is afraid of being found out. His wife taunts him by saying that if he is a real man, he'll go through with it. That night Macbeth murders Duncan. Then Lady Macbeth plants the murder weapons, the knives, on Duncan's sleeping attendants. When the murder is discovered, Macbeth kills the attendants so that there are no possible witnesses. Duncan's sons, Malcolm and Donalbain, flee for safety to England and to Ireland.

The effects of a guilty conscience

MACBETH is the most powerful **thane**. He will become king now that MALCOLM has fled. But he has no peace or security. To make sure that THE WITCHES' **prophecy** that BANQUO will be the founder of a line of kings will not come true, Macbeth gives orders to have Banquo and his son FLEANCE murdered. The killers succeed in killing Banquo, but Fleance escapes.

At a grand feast for all the court, Macbeth sees Banquo's ghost and is terrified. LADY MACBETH tries to cover up Macbeth's tell-tale and strange behaviour, but finally she has to send everyone home before his guilt becomes obvious. Relations between the husband and wife are strained as Macbeth retreats into a state of terror.

The witches' prediction

Macbeth turns to the witches again for help. They conjure up a parade of future kings. They are all descendants of Banquo. The only comfort for Macbeth is the witches' promise that he will be king until Birnam Wood moves towards his castle of Dunsinane. He is also told that "none of woman born" can kill him.

As woods do not move and all men are born of women, Macbeth thinks he is safe. But he goes on killing to remove all opposition. His murderers swoop on the defenseless family of MACDUFF, who is in England with Malcolm.

ABOVE: American John Singer Sargent painted this portrait of actress Ellen Terry as Lady Macbeth in London in 1888.

Malcolm forms an army

At the English court, Macduff asks Malcolm to raise an army and win back the throne. Malcolm is cautious, but when he sees Macduff's despair at the thought that there is no good man to lead Scotland, he admits that he has already negotiated an army with the English king. They agree to set out together to attack Macbeth. The THANE OF ROSS arrives. He tells Macduff that his family is dead. Macduff's grief turns to anger.

Lady Macbeth despairs

Lady Macbeth's nerves crack. She has nightmares. She talks about the murder as she sleepwalks. She washes imaginary blood from her hands.

The Scottish thanes opposed to Macbeth meet up with the army led by Malcolm and Macduff. Macbeth is defiant, but almost at once things begin to go wrong. He is told that his wife has killed herself. Then a messenger arrives to tell him that Birnam Wood appears to be moving towards the castle. What has actually happened is that the advancing English army has camouflaged itself with branches. Macbeth senses disaster but rushes out to face his enemies.

Macbeth is killed

Macbeth meets young SIWARD, son of the Earl of Northumberland. They fight, and the young man is killed. But then he comes up against Macduff. He taunts Macduff with the witches' prophecy that "none of woman born" can kill him. Macduff replies that he was not "of woman born", but delivered by **Caesarean section**. They fight, and Macbeth is killed.

After the battle, Macduff returns to Malcolm with Macbeth's head, so all can see that the tyrant is dead. The thanes proclaim Malcolm king. He promises a new peace for Scotland.

BELOW: Macbeth and the witches summon up the spirits in this scene from the Royal Shakespeare Company, 2004.

The themes

Shakespeare wrote four plays that are known as **tragedies**: *Hamlet*, *Othello*, *King Lear*, and *Macbeth*. Each of these shows the decline of the hero from a position of security to a position of **catastrophe**. The suffering unleashed leads to the hero's death and affects everyone else.

Shakespeare's tragedies look at the dark depths of human experience. They are about betrayal, cruelty, jealousy, ambition, power, murder, and revenge. These plays are not comfortable to read or watch. There is little sense of justice and little hope. Many characters suffer far more than they seem to deserve. The plays raise many questions. How much are we responsible for our own actions or are we victims of blind fate? What is good and evil? What are the consequences of behaving well or behaving badly?

Choice

Macbeth is a play about choice. It spotlights human beings on the edge. Decisions are made. Consequences unfold. Human action causes a chain of events. But there is also a larger, more mysterious and frightening aspect to the world of this play. The supernatural keeps breaking through, often in terrifying and violent forms. There are times when MACBETH seems a victim as well as a tyrant.

Fate

Macbeth and BANQUO are told by the witches that certain things will happen, but not how these things will happen. They are given no hint of the consequences. Must Macbeth take action in order to be king? Will he be a good or a bad king?

BELOW: This production of *Macbeth* is set in London during World War 1. It includes the young Laurence Olivier, fourth from the right, one of the most famous Shakespearian actors of the 20th century.

Could Macbeth turn his back on the **WEIRD** SISTERS and reject what they are offering? In other words, can Macbeth choose, or have the decisions already been made? And later, when LADY MACBETH taunts him with cowardice for his reluctance to kill DUNCAN, is she acting with her eyes wide open, fully aware of the consequences, or is she, too, at the mercy of a blind, evil fate?

Of course it might be that the Weird Sisters recognized Macbeth's ambition. They knew that some people cannot resist the temptations of gaining and keeping power. As Banquo says to them,

My noble partner
You greet with present grace
and great prediction
Of noble having and of royal hope,
That he seems rapt withal.
To me you speak not.

How far are the Macbeths responsible for what they do? In the end Shakespeare seems to say that we must all take responsibility for our actions. There are temptations and opportunities and there are parts of our characters and our relationships with others that seem to take us down certain paths. Yet we can always choose. How many people would turn away from the knowledge that Macbeth is given by the Weird Sisters?

Macbeth's conscience never lets him forget the difference between what he should have done and what he did do. He should have been a loyal subject of King Duncan. He should have accepted MALCOLM as heir. He should not have killed the King. But he gave way to Lady Macbeth's goading and her belief that they would get away with their misdeeds. He suffers the torments of conscience. He is troubled by the questions of what is right and what is wrong.

RIGHT: Macbeth (Derek Jacobi) and Lady Macbeth (Cheryl Campbell) have Duncan's blood on their hands in a Royal Shakespeare Company production in 1994.

Appearance and reality

MACBETH and LADY MACBETH embark on a career of murder because they have convinced themselves that Macbeth should be king. But as Macbeth carries out more murders to become king, there is a great gap between the confident way he and his wife must appear in public and their private world of fear and guilt.

When Lady Macbeth urges her husband to kill DUNCAN, she thinks they can leave their consciences behind. But she is mistaken. From the beginning, Macbeth knows that what he is doing is wrong. For a time his ambition lets him ignore his wrongful actions, but in the end, he is wracked with guilt.

A world of opposites

The imagery of the play is often about pairs of opposites. There is night and day; darkness and light; sleeplessness and sleep; and the "devilish" Macbeth and the saintly King of England. The play is also about confusion.

Fair is foul and foul is fair

and

So fair and foul a day I have not seen.

By their actions, Macbeth and his wife plunge themselves and Scotland into a nightmare, where what should be clear is actually confused.

BELOW: Yukio Ninagawa's production was staged at London's National Theatre in 1987.

This confusion is powerfully expressed in the banquet scene following Macbeth's coronation where BANQUO's ghost appears to the new king. There is great dramatic tension between Lady Macbeth's efforts to continue with the formal celebration and Macbeth's terror at being confronted by his murderous actions.

Macbeth is trapped by his guilty conscience, and at times, Lady Macbeth cannot escape her feelings of pity. For her husband's sake, she tries to push down any normal human emotion. For example, early in the play, she asks for all motherly feelings to be taken from her. But she still pities King Duncan and says that she would have killed him herself if he hadn't reminded her of her father. In the end, Lady Macbeth cannot live with herself. She has nightmares and she sleepwalks. She tries to wash imaginary blood from her hands.

> *... all the perfumes of Arabia will not sweeten this little hand.*

Neither Macbeth nor his wife can get the blood off their hands. In desperation, Lady Macbeth kills herself. As he hears of his wife's death, Macbeth realizes the futility of what he has done.

> *Life's but a walking shadow, a poor player*
> *That struts and frets his hour upon the stage,*
> *And then is heard no more.*

He faces his last battle with great courage.

BELOW: My hands are of your colour; but I shame to wear a heart so white." Judi Dench and Ian McKellen are Lady Macbeth and Macbeth in the 1976 Royal Shakespeare Company production.

PAST PRODUCTIONS

Oliver Cromwell and his **Puritan** government closed public theatres in 1642. With the restoration of the monarchy in 1660, two theatres were opened in London. Many of Shakespeare's plays returned to the stage. They were usually rewritten to meet changes in taste.

William Davenant's production of Macbeth included music and dancing, as well as "flying" WITCHES. This version remained popular until it was replaced by that of David Garrick, the most famous actor of his day. He first played MACBETH on 7 January, 1744. Although his production was nearer to Shakespeare's original than Davenant's, Garrick still made many changes. THE PORTER – omitted by Davenant on the grounds of bad taste – was replaced by "a respectable servant". The murders of LADY MACDUFF and her son were not shown. A long dying speech for Macbeth was added. This version of Macbeth was performed 96 times between 1744 and 1776, although Garrick's own last performance was on 22 September, 1768.

RIGHT: This scene with the witches, apparitions, Banquo's ghost, and Thomas Betterton as Macbeth is from a production of the 1600s.

Macbeth continued to be popular with audiences. Playing the central characters was seen as a great opportunity for actors to make an impact. At the beginning of the 1800s, Sarah Siddons played a legendary LADY MACBETH. Throughout the 19th century, the great actor-managers John Philip Kemble, Edmund Kean, William Macready, and Herbert Beerbohm Tree put on productions that fascinated the English with a romantic idea of Scotland. Instead of English military uniforms, the characters wore **tartan kilts** and carried **claymores**.

RIGHT: A painting by John Jackson shows a tartan-clad William Macready as Macbeth.

There has been a rich variety of productions of *Macbeth* in the 1900s. In 1921 in New York, Arthur Hopkins directed a version that was deliberately not realistic, but it was strong on atmosphere. Powerful beams of light cut across triangles and arches to suggest a frenzied world. Less successful was a 1926 London production that transferred the battlefields of the First World War to Scotland. At Stratford in 1936, Theodore Komisarjevsky's bold production included a set made from aluminum. His witches were old women who robbed bodies on the battlefield. BANQUO's ghost was done as Macbeth's shadow. In the same year in New York, Orson Welles set the play in Haiti. He used a cast of 130 African-American actors, and he included witch doctors and **voodoo**.

Orson Welles returned to the play again in 1948, this time in a movie. Other movies have included *Joe Macbeth* (1955), set in a Chicago gang war; and the Samurai *Throne of Blood*, directed by Akira Kurosawa in 1957. *Throne of Blood* explores the barbaric mind of Macbeth through striking visual images.

Shakespeare's story has also been the basis for three operas – one by Guiseppe Verdi in 1847, one by Ernst Bloch in 1910, and one by Dmitri Shostakovitch in 1934. Shostakovitch's *Lady Macbeth of the Mtsensk District* is built on an interpretation of the character of Lady Macbeth. The heroine takes a lover, murders her husband, and then kills herself while being taken to a Siberian prison. Its bleak plot adapts the themes of Shakespeare's tragedy to the lives of Russian peasants. **Tragedy** is not just for kings and lords.

The strangest production of all was Barbara Gerson's 1966 adaptation called *Macbird!* This production imagined similarities between the assassinations of KING DUNCAN and President John F. Kennedy.

Macbeth is one of Shakespeare's most frequently performed plays around the world. Its themes never fail to interest actors, directors, and audiences.

ACTORS' PERSPECTIVES
• playing Macbeth •

Like tragic heroes, actors make choices. In Shakespeare's *Macbeth*, one of the first and biggest choices an actor must make is to decide what MACBETH's state of mind is just before he meets the witches for the first time. Is he already ambitious the to be king? Or is the message of the **WEIRD** SISTERS a whole new idea? Many other decisions follow. What are Macbeth's attitudes towards BANQUO, his superstition, and especially, his relationship with LADY MACBETH.

David Garrick

When an actor plays Macbeth and also directs the play, as David Garrick did in 1744, he has even more choices of how to play the role. He might even change the **text**, too. In the 1700s, people thought it was all right to change the text. But today, it is unlikely that anyone would make changes, such as adding a dying speech at the end.

Garrick made changes, which made his Macbeth a murderer and a tyrant whose conscience eventually catches up with him.

Garrick's Macbeth was undoubtedly on the way to hell. In his dying speech, he says, "It is too late, hell drags me down. I sink ... "

LEFT: An 18th-century engraving of David Garrick as Macbeth.

Garrick's Macbeth was intended to provide an important moral lesson for the audience. The lesson was "This is what happens to the wicked". Those watching may have felt pity as Garrick died on the two-metre (six-foot) square, green carpet that was provided for all death scenes at this time. They would also have felt terror. Hell was, for them, a reality.

An audience today is unlikely to see Macbeth's journey towards **catastrophe** in terms of heaven and hell. But there is a big question to ask about tragic heroes. Is their destruction and the destruction of those around them a waste of human potential? What did Macbeth fail to achieve that he could have achieved had he remained a loyal subject of KING DUNCAN? One of the big issues of the play is how much sympathy can the audience feel for Macbeth.

Laurence Olivier

One of the greatest actors in the 1900s was Laurence Olivier. He tackled the role of Macbeth twice. He also played the role of MALCOLM in the 1926 production that was set during the first World War. He was particularly admired for his performance in the Stratford season of 1955. Critics of the time give a memorable picture of Olivier. They said, "... he radiates a kind of brooding sinister energy ... " Olivier's Macbeth was a man haunted by the thought of murder right from the start. The **WEIRD** SISTERS" **prophecy** stoked a fire of ruthless ambition, which was already lit.

BELOW: This is a portrait by Ruskin Spear of Laurence Olivier as Macbeth in 1955.

Ian McKellen

Twenty years later at Stratford, Ian McKellen also gave a performance that showed the inner progress of a man driven to power. At first, Ian McKellen's MACBETH was firmly in control of his public self. Macbeth was able to play the part of a loyal subject of KING DUNCAN. But the public mask began to crack and slip away. It was as if the gap between how he was seen by others and his murderous private world was too great for him to hold together. After murdering Duncan, he stared at his own bloody hands with disbelief. Macbeth was appalled at what he had done.

McKellen was superb in the banquet scene when he portrayed Macbeth's shock of seeing BANQUO's ghost. He collapsed with an epileptic fit. Gradually Macbeth's private world began to fall apart as well, and he turned to the **WEIRD** SISTERS.

Desperate to know about the future, Macbeth was given only dolls and puppets. These are the sad little charms and talismans of witchcraft. He carried them with him even into the final battle with MACDUFF. One theatre critic summed up Ian McKellen's performance as a "study of evil bursting through a mask, like a clown through a paper hoop".

Jonathan Pryce

When director Adrian Noble began working on the play in 1986, he had a company of actors led by Jonathan Pryce and Sinead Cusack. Noble wanted to play down the supernatural idea in order to explore the character's inner desires. The actors researched case studies of murderers. They tried to understand the murderers' state of mind.

Jonathan Pryce has said that in preparing for the role, he was aware of the political situation in which Macbeth acts. He remembered that in Scotland, the crown did not automatically pass from father to son. Instead, the symbol of kingship went to the **thane**, or lord, who was best able to rule. Macbeth saves his country in battle. He is an honoured member of the King's **Court**. He is, in fact, a suitable successor to the throne. So it is not surprising that he is disappointed when Duncan makes MALCOLM his heir. It is possible to see Macbeth as having both personal and patriotic reasons for claiming the crown. Perhaps he is the best man to rule Scotland.

By remembering this during rehearsal, an actor might see Macbeth as a complex figure. He would not be a simply evil or psychopathic character, even though he commits evil deeds. As Jonathan Pryce said, "Maybe one would say they were evil, but that evil was part of their political system".

Derek Jacobi

The darkness and fear that is such an important part of the play's atmosphere means that Macbeth can work very well in small theatre spaces. It was performed in 1999 by the Royal Shakespeare Company in the intimacy of the Swan Theatre. The actors were encouraged by the director, Gregory Doran, to think of the most frightening moment in their lives and bring that into their performance. Sir Antony Sher played Macbeth as a modern and strong war hero. And this production was particularly good at detailing the Macbeth's marriage. They loved each other, but something was missing.

LEFT: Macbeth (Jonathan Pryce) faces the last battle in Adrian Noble's 1986 production.

ACTORS' PERSPECTIVES
• playing Lady Macbeth •

If MACBETH's character is a frightening prospect for an actor, then LADY MACBETH is even more challenging. After only a few minutes on stage, the actress has the extraordinary speech in which Lady Macbeth calls on supernatural powers to strip her of all womanly qualities, replacing them with "direst cruelty". She is committed to her violent purpose. There will be no pity, no shrinking from whatever horrors become necessary. The speech is a terrifying spell. It conjures up evil power. Perhaps it is not surprising that some actresses have shied away from expressing such dangerous thoughts. Yet Lady Macbeth is also an irresistible challenge for an actress.

Sarah Siddons

The great actress, Sarah Siddons (1755–1831), described her own unnerving experience as a young actress first approaching the part of Lady Macbeth.

I shut myself up as usual, when all the family were retired, and commenced my study of Lady Macbeth. I went on with tolerable composure [quite calmly], in the silence of the night, till I came to the assassination scene, when the horrors of the scene rose to a degree that made it impossible to get farther. I snatched up my candle, and hurried out of the room in a paroxysm [fit] of terror.

RIGHT: This painting by Thomas Beach in 1806 shows Sarah Siddons as Lady Macbeth, John Philip Kemble plays Macbeth.

Sarah Siddons went on to score one of her greatest acting triumphs. She impressed her audiences with her portrayal of a superbly intelligent, powerful, and mesmerizing Lady Macbeth. Those who saw it would never forget the sleep-walking scene in which Lady Macbeth acts out the murder once again and pretends to pour water desperately over her hands. For one onlooker it was all very real. He wrote, "Well, sir, I smelt blood! I swear I smelt blood."

Audiences today are probably harder to convince than those who flocked to see Sarah Siddons. We are more used to a realistic style of acting in movies and on television. Any hint of **melodrama** would ruin a modern actress's portrayal of Lady Macbeth.

Judi Dench

Judi Dench played the role at Stratford in 1976, opposite Ian McKellen's Macbeth. She found the character's motivation in Lady Macbeth's ambition for her husband, as well in the ambition for herself. Her motives were a twisted form of her love for him. She was attracted by the black magic he became involved in, and she dabbled in satanic practices. Bur she was also afraid, fainting to the ground at the end of the banquet scene where Macbeth sees Banquo's ghost.

RIGHT: Judi Dench played Lady Macbeth and Ian McKellen played Macbeth for the Royal Shakespeare Company in 1976.

Her husband picked her up and pushed her face into a normal expression as if she were a puppet or a ventriloquist's dummy. Lady Macbeth was then ready for the next public performance.

This understanding of Lady Macbeth, linking her intimately with her husband, was one which Judi Dench made convincingly strong. She appeared capable of everything vicious, but at the same time she was vulnerable. Once Macbeth retreated into his own world of terror and tyranny, she was totally lost. She had no purpose; to continue after that, and her death "at her own hand" comes as no surprise.

The Macbeths' relationship

How the director sees the relationship between the Macbeths affects his choice of the cast. Many directors have wanted to indicate a strong love between the two, which LADY MACBETH uses when she goads her husband into killing KING DUNCAN.

Helen Mirren played a young and sexy Lady Macbeth in the 1974 Royal Shakespeare Company production, with Nicol Williamson as a satanic MACBETH. This Lady Macbeth used her sexuality to goad the ambitious Macbeth on to murder.

A highly stylized Japanese language version of the play, directed by Yukio Ninagawa, visited the National Theatre in London in 1987. The production seemed to tilt the play away from the harsh masculine world, in which it so often takes place, towards a much more feminine world. This was accentuated by the constant fall of cherry blossoms. Komaki Kurihara's beauty and fragility as Lady Macbeth covered up an ambition that at first appalled Macbeth and then turned him into a willing puppet of her manipulation. She showed the close links that there can be between sexual attractiveness and a desire for power.

Sinead Cusack

Sinead Cusack played Lady Macbeth in Adrian Noble's 1986 production for the Royal Shakespeare Company. The director encouraged her and Jonathan Pryce, as her husband, to explore the ordinariness of evil. How can great evil grow from comparatively small and simple choices and attitudes?

The two actors looked at their relationship as Mr. and Mrs. Macbeth, rather than the **Thane** of Glamis and his Lady. They began before the play starts, imagining how the Macbeths would already have been plotting, talking about the succession to the throne, convincing each other that Macbeth was the best man for the job. Sinead Cusack did not portray Lady Macbeth as a mean woman, but as a woman obsessed by her husband. Sinead felt that at some time the couple had lost their child, and, in their pain, had turned in towards each other.

Sinead Cusack's Lady Macbeth was totally ambitious for her husband, but she didn't think about where this ambition would lead them. Again and again, she made wrong choices. She thought that asking to have all feelings of pity removed from her and to exercise "direst cruelty" would be enough. She thought that she would be able to share in the killing of Duncan. But, in the end, she could not live with it. Her feelings came back to haunt her.

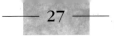

Sinead Cusack, and Jonathan Pryce in particular, showed how the Macbeths began as a couple, but by the end they were facing their own individual hells. For Sinead Cusack, this was seen most crucially in the killing of Duncan. Lady Macbeth, she came to feel, was completely possessed by the excitement of listening to her husband plunging the daggers into the sleeping king. They entered hell together. But from this moment, they started to go their separate ways. Lady Macbeth had unlocked something in her husband for which she had not bargained. The one killing gave Macbeth the urge to do many more killings. For his wife, the first killing led to horror, disintegration, and finally suicide.

ABOVE: Harriet Walter played Lady Macbeth in the Royal Shakespeare Company's 1999 production.

THE WEIRD SISTERS AND THE PORTER

One of the most exciting things about exploring Shakespeare's plays is the way he makes important ideas reappear in so many unlikely forms. *Macbeth* is a play of extremes and opposites. This can be seen in the images: night and day, darkness and light, and so on. The extremes and opposites are in the contrasts between good kings and wicked tyrants, and in the mutually destructive relationship of MACBETH and LADY MACBETH. Extremes are in the list of characters itself – the **WEIRD** SISTERS and the PORTER.

At first look, there seems little connection between three witches, who give mysterious **prophecies** and conjure up supernatural powers, and a drunken gatekeeper with his leering humour and the original "Knock, knock ... " jokes. But in *Macbeth* opposites tend to meet. The witches represent evil and companions to the devil, and the Porter is really the keeper of the gates of hell. All represent the forces of darkness that conquer the Macbeths.

Everyone knows there are witches in *Macbeth*. Many people could quote their chanting from the opening scenes. "When shall we three meet again ... ", and the chant from act 4, "Double, double, toil and trouble ... " What seems familiar now was very frightening to Shakespeare's audiences. What is the purpose of the witches?

In many early productions, they were part of a spectacle. In the 1600s and 1700s, they sang and danced and even flew from wires hanging above the stage. In a world that still believed in the power of witchcraft, perhaps that was necessary as a way of making their dangers less disturbing.

RIGHT: These are the Weird Sisters as painted by Johann Heinrich Fuseli.

In many productions in the 1900s, they became more human. For example, they are portrayed as old women searching the battlefields for treasures. But the challenge of *Macbeth* is to make the Weird Sisters both human and strange, believable yet terrifying, all at the same time.

Trevor Nunn's production in 1976 placed the witches in a world where they would be believed and feared. The third witch, a young woman speaking like a spiritualist's **medium**, sees visions that terrify her, and the audience is taken into her own frantic imagination. Later, when Macbeth asked for more visions, the witches used childish things, dolls and puppets, to summon up the spirits.

This connection of the witches with children was taken even further in Adrian Noble's 1986 production. Here the third witch had a child of her own. This contrasted with Macbeth, whose own child was dead. Later, the ghostly apparitions Macbeth asks for were again children, who then became MACDUFF'S children, who were murdered at Macbeth's command. It was as if Macbeth was haunted by his childlessness. Not having children puts the Macbeths in their own despairing hell.

Sometimes the actor playing the Porter is encouraged to ad-lib (inventing lines which are not in Shakespeare's text). In the 1999 RSC production, for example, Stephen Noonan, playing the Porter, made up jokes about the Prime Minister, Tony Blair. The Porter has a practical role: he speaks long enough for the Macbeths to wash the blood from their hands. But he is also like the devil – and his jokes are about deceit, truth, and falsehood – the major themes of the play. The Macbeths have welcomed DUNCAN under their roof as loyal subjects and honest hosts. Now they have killed him. With their murderous deception, they have entered the hell whose gates the Porter will now open. It is a hell they will never leave.

RIGHT: "Knock. knock, knock. Who's there? An equivocator." Ian McDiarmid is the comic Porter for the Royal Shakespeare Company of 1976.

GLOSSARY

Caesarean section operation in which a baby is removed from the uterus by cutting through a woman's abdomen

catastrophe disastrous end, usually bringing death or ruin to the leading character in a play

claymore heavy, two-edged sword used by Scottish Highlanders

court family, household, or followers of a king, queen, or member of the royal family

depose put out of office or position of authority

Elizabethan relating to Queen Elizabeth I of England and her reign, from 1533–1603

frontispiece illustration facing the title page of a book

heath open land with low bushes but few or no trees

kilt pleated knee-length skirt worn by men in the Scottish Highlands

Lord Chamberlain royal official responsible for the entertainment at Court

medium person through whom messages from spirits are said to be sent to the living

melodrama sensational drama that is exaggerated and appeals to the emotions

playhouse theatre

prophecy telling of future events

Puritan Protestant who felt that personal responsibility and moral purity were very necessary to Christian life

rebellion fight against one's government

tartan checked, woollen cloth

text original words of an author

thane baron or a lord in Scottish history

tragedy form of a play that shows the downfall of a hero and the suffering and death that the downfall creates

voodoo religion made up of mysterious rites and practices that include magic and conjuring

weird from the Old English word wyrd, meaning fate or destiny

MORE BOOKS TO READ

Macbeth, Linda Buckle (ed.)
(Cambridge School Shakespeare, 2004)

Eyewitness guides: Shakespeare, Peter Chrisp
(Dorling Kindersley, 2004)

The life and world of William Shakespeare, Struan Reid
(Heinemann Library, 2004)

WEBSITES

These websites give a great deal of useful information:

www.shakespeare.org.uk
The website of the Shakespeare Birthplace Trust. Contains biographical information on Shakespeare and educational resources on his work.

www.rsc.org.uk
The website of the Royal Shakespeare Company. Includes a wealth of information about performances past and present.

www.shakespeares-globe.org
The website of the Globe Theatre in London. Features information about the building and performances. You can also find details of educational resources available.

INDEX

A
ambition 5, 11, 14, 16, 20

B
BANQUO 6–8, 10–12,
   14, 15, 17–20, 22, 25
Buchanan, George 7

Chamberlain, Lord 4
Chamberlain's Men 4, 5
conscience 5, 7, 11, 12,
   15–17, 20
Cusack, Sinead 22, 26, 27

D
Daemonologie 4, 5
Davenant, William 18
Dench, Judi 25
Doran, Gregory 23
DUNCAN 6, 8, 10, 11,
   15–17, 19, 21, 22, 26,
   27, 29

E
Elizabeth I 4, 6
evil 5, 14, 22, 26, 28

F
fate 14
Forman, Simon 7

G
Garrick, David 18, 20, 21
Globe Theatre 4, 7
guilt 5, 7, 12, 16, 17
Gunpowder Plot 5

H
Holinshed's *Chronicles* 6, 7

J
James I 4, 5, 6, 7

K
Kean, Edmund 18
Kemble, J.P. 18
Kennedy, John F. 19
King's Men 5
Komisarjevsky, Theodore
   19
Kurahira, Komaki 26
Kurosawa, Akira 19

L
LADY MACBETH 7, 8, 11,
   12, 13, 15–17, 20, 24,
   25, 28, 29
LADY MACDUFF 12, 18

M
MACBETH (character) 6, 7,
   10–14, 16–29
Macbeth (opera) 19
Macbeth (play) 5, 7, 8,
   10–14, 18, 19, 28, 29
Macbird! (play) 19
MACDUFF 12, 13, 23, 29
Macready, William 18
MALCOLM 11, 13, 15, 21,
   22
McKellen, Ian 22, 25
Mirren, Helen 26

N
Ninagawa, Yukio 26
Noble, Adrian 22, 23, 26,
   29
Noonan, Stephen 29
Nunn, Trevor 29

P
PORTER 9, 18,29
Pryce Jonathan 22, 23, 26,
   27

S
Seneca 7
Shakespeare, William 4–7
Sher, Sir Antony 23
Siddons, Sarah 18, 24, 25

T
Throne of Blood 19
tragedy 14, 19, 21
Tree, Herbert Beerbohm
   18

W
WEIRD SISTERS 5, 7, 8, 10,
   14,15, 20–23, 28, 29
Welles, Orson 19
Williamson, Nicol 26
witches and witchcraft 5, 22